Sigma Unbound

Breaking the Mold

Beyond Alpha and Beta:

The Sigma Male and Sigma Female's Guide to Personal Power

Disclaimers

1. The author makes no guarantees concerning the level of success you may experience by following the advice and strategies contained in this book, and you accept the risk that results will differ for each individual. The examples provided in this book show exceptional results, which may not apply to the average reader, and are not intended to represent or guarantee that you will achieve the same or similar results.

2. Before we plunge deep into the nuanced world of Sigmas, it's crucial to clarify a point that lies at the heart of this exploration. Although this book frequently references 'Sigma male,' the principles, struggles, and triumphs discussed are not confined to a single gender. The Sigma

traits—autonomy, mastery, and depth of thought—are universal, transcending gender boundaries. Therefore, Sigma females, or Sigma women who identify with these qualities, will also find relevance and validation in these pages. This book aims to be a guide for all who see themselves as the architects of their path, regardless of gender. So, whether you've always known you're a Sigma or are just beginning to explore this aspect of your identity, welcome.

Introduction

In the vast canvas of human existence, where conformity often weaves the threads of societal expectations, there emerges a distinct silhouette—a figure that moves to the rhythm of its own heartbeat, unbound by the chains of conventionality. This figure, this archetype, is the Sigma Male. Welcome to "Sigma Unbound: Breaking the Mold."

Defying Definition, Embracing Individuality

"Sigma Male" isn't just a classification; it's a declaration of independence and a manifesto of uniqueness. In a world that often seeks to categorize and pigeonhole, sigma males rise as the embodiment of autonomy—a force that cannot be contained within the boxes society creates. As we embark on this exploration, consider this not merely a book but a journey into the essence of breaking molds and living unapologetically.

The Call of Sigma Unbound

"Sigma Unbound" is more than a title; it's a rallying cry for those who dance to the beat of their own drum. This is an invitation to unravel the mysteries of the Sigma mindset, challenge the norms that attempt to stifle individuality and to embrace the unconventional path that leads to genuine freedom.

In the chapters that follow, we will traverse the landscapes of independence, exploring the power found within solitude, the mastery of social dynamics, the realm of personal empowerment, and the intricate dance of relationships on sigma terms. We'll navigate the uncharted territories of crafting a life beyond societal expectations and achieving success on terms defined by the individual.

A Manifesto for the Unconventional

As we dive into "Sigma Unbound," imagine it as a manifesto—a proclamation that celebrates the unseen strengths of the Sigma male. Each word, each chapter, is an assertion of the power that resides within the individual who refuses to conform, who thrives in the shadows, and who revels in the art of breaking the mold.

This book is not just about understanding the Sigma male; it's about unleashing the Sigma within you. It's about recognizing that true power lies not in conformity but in the audacity to authentically be yourself. "Sigma Unbound" challenges you to question, to rebel, and to embrace the rebel spirit that resides within every Sigma male.

The Unveiling Begins

As we embark on this expedition into the realms of Sigma Unbound, prepare to have preconceptions shattered, norms questioned, and limitations dismantled. Together, we will uncover the wisdom, the strength, and the artistry that define the sigma male experience.

So, fellow rebels, let the journey into "Sigma Unbound: Breaking the Mold" commence. Let the pages turn, the ideas unfold, and the rebel spirit rise. This is not just a book; it's a call to unbind, to redefine, and to celebrate the extraordinary journey of being a true Sigma male.

Chapter 1: Embracing Independence: The Unapologetic Path of the Sigma

In the realm of social hierarchies, where Alphas and Betas dance in a predictable ballet of dominance and submission, Sigmas stand apart. If you're reading this, chances are you're one of us—a lone wolf, a renegade who doesn't just step out of line but questions why the line exists in the first place.

Let's just cut the bullshit. This isn't about being a wallflower with a secret superiority complex. It's about acknowledging that the traditional path trodden by the masses isn't just unappealing to you; it's fucking suffocating. It's about the deep, guttural need to carve out your own space in this world, rules be damned.

Being a Sigma isn't a quiet resignation from societal games; it's a bold, loud declaration of independence. It's the realization that fitting in is overrated and that standing out doesn't mean standing alone. It's about finding your tribe—those few who get it, who understand the fire that burns within you, the relentless drive to live on your terms. When we talk about being happy alone, it's not because friends aren't good. Friends are great! But sometimes, it's ok to be realistic. You need to also know how to be alone, they can't and won't always be there. It's part of life.

Think about Vincent van Gogh, the famous painter. Even when he was by himself, he could make amazing, elaborate pictures that still wow people today. It's like when you were a kid and created an awesome drawing or building block castle on your own. That's one of the purest forms of celebrating by yourself and making the best out of it, which is our first big idea.

Leonardo da Vinci, the painter of the Mona Lisa, liked to think and work by himself a lot. He came up with his cool inventions and beautiful paintings because we knew how to spend time alone with his ideas. It's like having a secret clubhouse, or a special nook where you come up with brilliant plans or plot your adventures, like the Bat Cave.

Learning to be on your own is the key to a treasure chest full of the good shyt. It's not for anyone; it's for the kids in us who are curious beyond the playground and the grown-ups who love to learn and apply. Take this time to see that being by yourself doesn't mean you're lonely; it means you're strong and full of ideas, ready to explore the world in your own special way.

This path isn't for the faint-hearted. It demands resilience, the courage to face your darkness, and the audacity to live authentically in a world that constantly tries to fit you into neatly labeled boxes. It's about being unapologetically you, in a world that often rewards conformity over individuality.

You're not here to be liked. You're here to make a fucking statement. To live a life that's unabashedly yours. That means making choices that won't always win you friends but will always keep you true to yourself. It's about the satisfaction of knowing you're not playing by anyone else's rules but your own.

This isn't an invitation to nihilism or a call to anarchic rebellion. It's an awakening to the profound power of self-sufficiency. It's about cultivating a deep-seated confidence that comes from knowing you can rely on yourself, and that you are your best resource.

We leave behind the idea that you always need others to have fun or be interesting and step into a world where being on your own is like being the hero of your journey. Turn your "me time" into a superpower.

Here's the deal: if you're ready to dive headfirst into the depths of what it means to live as a Sigma, to embrace the solitude, the introspection, and the sheer exhilarating terror of making your way, then you're in the right place. This journey is about unleashing the potent force of your individuality, about becoming so fucking authentic that the world can't help but stop and take notice.

Chapter 2: Mastering Social Dynamics: The Sigma's Playbook

Fresh off the high of embracing your unyielding independence, you might wonder, "Where do I fit in the grand scheme of social dynamics?" Let's get this straight: just because we thrive in solitude doesn't mean we're clueless hermits. Far from it. Understanding and navigating social landscapes are where we, as Sigmas, excel—it's our secret weapon, our ace in the hole.

Here's the thing: we're not anti-social; we're selectively social. And there's a profound power in that selectivity. It's not about shunning society but engaging with it on our terms, understanding its rules well enough to bend them to our will. It's playing the game without becoming another pawn on the board.

Even superheroes need a little time alone sometimes. Just like Batman, who's good at fighting bad guys, but he also knows how to be alone and think up clever plans to save the day. That's what we call being selective about when you want to be around others and when you need some time to yourself.

Now moving through social circles as a Sigma isn't about manipulation or deceit. It's about authentic connection on our own terms. It's knowing that every interaction doesn't need to lead to a lifelong friendship but can still be meaningful. It's about leaving a mark, and making an impact without the need for constant presence.

The key to mastering social dynamics as a Sigma lies in strategic engagement. It's about identifying the interactions that add value to your life and those that drain you. It's investing energy wisely, in relationships that matter, in networks that empower you, while gracefully bowing out from those that don't align with your path.

Think of it as being the director of your own social script. You choose the cast, the scenes, and the interactions that make up the epic tale of your life. It's about being present without being pervasive, influential without being invasive.

And let's debunk a myth right here: Sigmas are not lacking in charisma. In fact, our charisma is like a sniper's aim—precise, deliberate, and impactful.

It's not about being the loudest in the room but the most memorable. It's the art of subtle influence, of leaving people feeling better for having crossed paths with you, even if those encounters are few and far between.

Here's your playbook for mastering social dynamics: observe, engage, influence, and retreat. It's a dance, and you're the one leading, moving in and out of the social spotlight at will, always on your own terms.

So, as we dive deeper into the nuances of social interactions, remember this: your solitude is your strength, but your ability to navigate the social maze is your superpower. Embrace it, wield it wisely, and watch as the world bends to the rhythm of your unique dance.

Chapter 3: Carving Your Destiny: No Room for Half-Measures

Welcome to the raw, unfiltered heart of your journey. This is where the rubber meets the road, where you look at the neatly laid plans of society and say, "Fuck that, I'm going my own way." It's not just about walking a solitary path; it's about slashing through the brambles and underbrush with your will as your machete. It's about demanding more from life and refusing to settle for the pre-packaged bullshit they sell as "success."

Think about explorers like Indiana Jones. He didn't follow a map someone else made; he was all about creating his own map, discovering hidden treasures, and going on adventures no one else had dreamed of. That's what carving your destiny is all about—finding your own treasures in life, even if it means going places where there are no paths yet.

Ay man, say man, imagine you're working on one of those big-ass puzzles with hundreds of pieces. Some people might try to copy someone else's way of solving it, but you decide to put it together in a way that makes sense to you, and suddenly, you see the picture before anyone else does. That's you, being smart and creative, making your own decisions. It's your puzzle, work it your way.

Be brave and bold! You decide what games you want to play! What puzzles do you want to solve? What adventures do you want to go on? Stop letting people pick out your damn puzzles for you! You're grown! Hell, I don't even let anyone see my puzzle till it's done. My mom doesn't even know that I'm writing this book. Nothing against my mom, I'm just used to moving in silence. (Hey, Ma)

Let's get something straight: sharing your journey or showing your cards isn't always a smart move overall. Think of your path as a high-stakes poker game; showing your hand too soon is a surefire way to get played. The world, as much as we wish it were different, is brimming with envy and silent adversaries. These are the shadows that lurk, waiting to douse your flames the moment they catch a whiff of your fire.

There's power in silence, in the covert grind, in the unseen battles you fight every day to bring your visions to life. Why? Because while everyone else is busy talking about what they're going to do, you're doing it. By the time they catch on, you're already miles ahead, unveiling the masterpiece you've poured your soul into. This isn't about disdain for others; it's about safeguarding your essence, your creative spirit, from the parasites of pessimism and the doubters who feast on dreams—I guarantee you know who a few of them are.

Remember, the most significant accomplishments often emerge from the shadows, not the spotlight. Protect your energy; let your results speak for themselves.

In a world that echoes with the clamor of empty promises and unfulfilled dreams, let the unveiling of your achievements be the thunder that silences the skeptics. Really fuck their heads up for sleeping on you, for doubting you, for not taking you seriously, for taking you for granted—all that. Let your success be the ultimate mindfuck, leaving them scratching their heads and wondering how they could have ever underestimated you. Keep your moves mysterious and let the impact of your actions reveal the depth of your journey. After all, nothing shuts down the naysayers like undeniable success, served cold and without warning.

Carving your destiny is an act of defiance. It's a spit in the face of conformity, a middle finger to the expectations that try to cage you. It's not for the timid or the indecisive. It's for the bold, the relentless, the unapologetically ambitious. It's for those who recognize that accountability isn't just a concept; it's the bedrock of true independence.

This chapter calls you out unapologetically. Truly ask yourself, are you a spectator or are you in the fucking game? It's easy to dream, to talk, to plan. But are you ready to bleed for what you want? Because let's get one thing straight: the path of a Sigma is paved with setbacks, failures, and heartbreaks. But every scar, every wound, is a badge of honor, proof that you're fighting the good fight and nothing has stopped you so far.

Accountability means owning your failures as fiercely as you claim your victories. It means looking in the mirror and acknowledging that if you don't like what you see, you've got the power to change it. No excuses, no blame-shifting. Just raw, unadulterated ownership of your life and your choices. No one is perfect; that 'L' was a Lesson. You can't lose what you never truly possessed.

Please understand that forging your own path isn't a solo death march. It's about knowing when to stand alone and when to draw strength from like-minded rebels who share your disdain for mediocrity. It's about being a beacon of raw, unyielding strength in a sea of half-hearted conformists.

This isn't a call to isolation; it's an invitation to lead. To take the uncharted route, light it up, and show others it's possible. It's about inspiring not by words, but by action. You're not just carving your destiny; you're laying down the gauntlet for others to pick up their swords and join the fray. The plain truth is the world doesn't need more sheep, aimlessly following. It needs Sigmas. It needs you, in all your defiant glory, to stand up and carve out a path that will leave a mark long after you're gone.

We're learning that to craft your own path, you don't need anyone else's permission. It's about listening to that little voice inside you that says, "Hey, let's try something different." It's like being a pirate on the open sea, looking for treasure, or a scientist discovering a new star. You're in charge, and the map you're drawing is yours alone.

This book isn't just stories and ideas; it's a compass pointing you toward your own adventures, showing you that the bravest thing you can do is be yourself and follow your own dreams.

Now, ask yourself, are you ready to own this journey? To commit to the grind, embrace the pain, and forge a legacy from the sweat of your brow and the strength of your will? Good. Because the world doesn't have time for half-measures. And frankly, neither do you.

Rise, Sigma. The world is yours for the taking. No apologies. No regrets. Just pure, unadulterated badassery. Let's fucking go.

Chapter 4: Embracing Resilience: Thriving in the Face of Adversity

In the battlefield of life, resilience is the armor that shields us from the blows of adversity. In this chapter, we're diving into the art of embracing resilience, a cornerstone of the Sigma mindset. We're not just talking about surviving tough times; we're talking about thriving in their midst, emerging from the crucible stronger and more determined than ever before.

Life has a way of throwing some pretty hefty sucker punches when we least expect them. But as Sigmas, we don't cower; we stand tall, unyielding in our resolve to overcome whatever challenges come our way. Whether it's a personal setback, a professional hurdle, or a global crisis, we refuse to be defeated. Instead, we rise to the occasion, drawing strength from within and pushing forward with unwavering determination.

Resilience isn't about pretending everything is fine when it's not. It's about facing your shit head-on, acknowledging the challenges we face, and finding the strength to overcome them. It's like playing a game of chess, where every move is strategic and calculated. We don't panic when our opponent makes a bold move; instead, we keep a cool head, assess the situation, and plan our next move with precision.

Resilience isn't just about weathering the storm; it's about thriving in its midst. It's about turning setbacks into opportunities, using every obstacle as a stepping stone to greater heights. It's about embracing the lessons that adversity teaches us, growing from our experiences, and emerging from the storm with newfound wisdom and strength.

Think of it like a mighty oak tree, weathering the fiercest storms with grace and resilience. Though the winds may howl and the rain may fall, the oak stands firm, its roots anchored deep in the earth. It bends, but it does not break, and when the storm passes, it stands even taller than before.

Resilience isn't just a trait that we're born with; it's also a skill that can be cultivated and strengthened over time. That's exactly what the Sigma male does. It starts with the mindset, with the belief that no matter how tough things get, we have the power to overcome. Proper preparation prevents poor performance. It's about cultivating a positive attitude, maintaining a sense of perspective, and refusing to let fear or doubt hold us back.

Next, it's about building a strong support network, surrounding ourselves with like-minded and goal-oriented people who lift us up and encourage us to keep moving forward. Whether it's friends, family, mentors, or peers, having a support system in place can make all the difference when times get tough.

And finally, it's about taking action, facing our challenges head-on and refusing to back down. It's about being proactive, seeking out solutions, and never losing sight of our goals, no matter how daunting the road ahead may seem.

So, my fellow Sigma, let's continue to embrace resilience as our greatest ally on the journey of life. Let's continue to face our challenges with courage, determination, and an unwavering belief in our ability to overcome. Let's continue to weather the storms with grace and strength, knowing that with resilience as our shield, there's no obstacle we can't conquer. Watch the board at all times. Sacrifice the Queen to save the King. She shouldn't have been out in traffic. Yeah, that was personal; every move a Sigma makes is personal.

As Sigmas, we don't just weather the storm; we dance in the rain, turning chaos into our canvas and adversity into our bitch.

Chapter 5: Cultivating Mastery: Becoming the Architect of Your Expertise

In this chapter, we're delving into the concept of cultivating mastery, a fundamental aspect of the Sigma mindset. Mastery isn't just about being good at something; it's about becoming the architect of your expertise, honing your skills to a razor-sharp edge, and wielding them with precision and finesse.

Much like Shakespeare meticulously crafted each line of his plays, shaping words into timeless works of art, mastering a skill requires dedication, attention to detail, and a commitment to excellence. Just as Sherlock Holmes meticulously observes his surroundings, noticing details that escape the average person, cultivating mastery empowers us to sharpen our senses and perceive nuances that others overlook.

As Sigmas, we're driven by a relentless pursuit of excellence, constantly pushing ourselves to reach new heights of skill and proficiency in our chosen endeavors. Whether it's mastering a musical instrument, perfecting a martial art, or becoming a master strategist, we refuse to settle for mediocrity. We strive for nothing less than greatness in everything we do.

This high level of mastery, though seemingly effortless, isn't achieved overnight; it's the result of years of dedicated practice, discipline, and the commitment of a Sigma on a scent, like white on rice, or a fly on shit. It's about embracing the grind, putting in the hours, and pushing past our limits, even when it feels like we've hit a plateau. It's about recognizing that failure is not the end but rather a necessary stepping stone on the path to success.

Imagine a sculptor chiseling away at a block of marble, patiently shaping and refining it until it becomes a masterpiece. Every strike of the chisel, every chip of the stone, brings us closer to our vision of perfection. And just like the sculptor, we must be willing to put in the work, to endure the challenges and setbacks that come with the creative process. Also like the sculptor, you will likely be the only one to see the result of what you're chipping away at, and that's fine.

But mastery is not just about technical skill; it's also about mindset. It's about cultivating a mindset of continuous growth and improvement, always striving to learn and evolve. It's about embracing feedback, both positive and negative, and using it to fuel our progress. It's about approaching every challenge with a sense of curiosity and openness, knowing that there's always more to learn and discover.

And perhaps most importantly, mastery is about finding joy and fulfillment in the journey itself. It's about embracing the process, savoring the small victories, and finding beauty in the struggle. It's about recognizing that true mastery is not a destination but a lifelong pursuit, a journey of self-discovery and self-expression.

So, my fellow Sigma, let's commit ourselves to the pursuit of mastery in everything we do. Let's embrace the grind, the challenges, and the setbacks, knowing that they are all essential parts of the journey. Let's cultivate a mindset of continuous growth and improvement, always pushing ourselves to reach new heights of excellence. And let's remember that true mastery is not just about what we achieve but who we become in the process.

We've bid farewell to the limitations of our past selves to embrace the boundless possibilities of our future. As our Sigma nature has it, we've stepped into a world where every challenge is an opportunity for growth, every setback a chance for resilience, and every success a testament to our inner strength.

Chapter 6: Navigating the Social Landscape: The Art of Strategic Connection

In this chapter, we're delving into the intricate dance of social dynamics, a realm where Sigmas excel with finesse and strategy. Navigating the social landscape isn't about being the life of the party or the center of attention; it's about understanding the power of strategic connection, forging alliances, and leveraging relationships to further our goals.

Imagine yourself as a master chess player, carefully plotting your moves and anticipating the actions of your opponents. That's the mindset of a Sigma navigating the social landscape. We're not interested in meaningless small talk or superficial interactions; we're focused on building meaningful connections with individuals who can add value to our lives and vice versa.

Just like Sherlock Holmes analyzes every detail of a crime scene, we're constantly observing and analyzing the people and situations around us. We're adept at reading between the lines, picking up on subtle cues and nuances that others may miss. This keen sense of observation allows us to tailor our interactions to suit the needs of the moment, whether it's charming a potential business partner or diffusing a tense situation.

But navigating the social landscape isn't just about manipulation or self-interest; it's about building genuine connections based on mutual respect and understanding. We approach every interaction with authenticity and integrity, never sacrificing our principles for the sake of expediency.

Navigating the realm of genuine connections can be akin to traversing uncharted territories, especially for those who dance to the beat of their own drum, like sigma individuals. It's not always easy, for we may not think the same, move the same, or express ourselves in conventional ways. Yet, it is precisely because of our unique perspectives and mannerisms that our connections hold such depth and richness.

As Sigmas, we recognize the value of our social network and invest in only mutually beneficial building relationships. Whether it's networking events, industry conferences, or social gatherings, we seize every opportunity to expand our circle of influence and connect with like-minded individuals who share our values and goals.

And just like a skilled diplomat, we know when to assert ourselves and when to step back, understanding that true power lies in influence, not dominance. We're masters of persuasion, able to sway opinions and win allies to our cause without resorting to coercion or manipulation.

In a world where social media dominates our interactions, we remain grounded in the timeless principles of human connection. We prioritize face-to-face communication and genuine engagement over likes and follows, recognizing that true relationships are built on trust and authenticity.

So, my fellow Sigma, let's continue to navigate the social landscape with grace and strategy.

Let's leverage our keen insight and strategic thinking to build meaningful connections and advance our goals. And let's never lose sight of the power of genuine human connection in an increasingly digital world.

Chapter 7: Cultivating Conscious Presence

In this pivotal chapter, we venture into the depths of self-awareness, a cornerstone of the Sigma mindset. Self-awareness isn't just about recognizing who we are; it's about fostering a conscious presence that permeates every aspect of our existence.

Picture yourself standing before a mirror, not merely observing your reflection but truly comprehending yourself—your aspirations, anxieties, strengths, and vulnerabilities. That's the essence of self-awareness—being attuned to the complexities of our inner world and embracing them with empathy and insight.

As Sigmas, we often find ourselves pausing to contemplate our actions and reactions, seeking to understand the underlying motives behind them. This practice empowers us to make deliberate choices and navigate life's challenges with clarity and resolve.

Imagine awakening each day with a clear understanding of your thoughts, emotions, and intentions. That's the power of self-awareness—a daily commitment to mindfulness and introspection, allowing us to navigate the intricacies of our own minds with grace and purpose.

In this chapter, we adopt the role of detectives, unraveling the mysteries of our own psyche and examining our beliefs, values, and biases with discernment. It's about acknowledging our imperfections and embracing them as integral facets of our identity.

Like skilled navigators charting a course through uncharted waters, we explore the vast expanse of our inner landscape, uncovering hidden truths and navigating turbulent seas with resilience and poise. We confront the shadows within us, recognizing that self-mastery begins with self-awareness.

Self-awareness is an ongoing journey—a commitment to self-exploration and growth that evolves with each passing day. Like tending to a garden, it requires patience, nurturing, and a willingness to embrace change.

As we journey through this chapter, we bid farewell to self-deception and embrace the liberating power of self-awareness. We step into a world where authenticity reigns supreme, where our actions are aligned with our values, and where we navigate life's complexities with integrity.

But self-awareness isn't a solitary endeavor; it's about cultivating awareness in our interactions with others. We listen deeply, empathize sincerely, and communicate authentically, recognizing that true connection begins with understanding ourselves and extending compassion to others.

This book serves as a roadmap for the journey of self-awareness, offering insights, reflections, and practical tools to deepen our understanding of ourselves and the world around us. Let it be a companion on your journey, revisited and shared with fellow seekers of truth.

So, my fellow Sigma, let's commit ourselves to the practice of self-awareness and the cultivation of conscious presence. Let's make it a daily ritual to pause, breathe, and tune in to the rhythm of our own hearts. In this pursuit of self-discovery, may we find true fulfillment and a deeper connection to ourselves and the world around us.

Chapter 8: Embracing Adaptability: Thriving in an Ever-Changing World

In this gritty chapter, we delve into the crucible of adaptability—a fundamental skill for Sigma individuals navigating the tumultuous seas of an ever-shifting world. While many cling desperately to familiarity and routine, Sigmas recognize that true strength lies in the ability to pivot, evolve, and flourish amidst uncertainty and chaos.

Adaptability isn't merely about rolling with the punches; it's about seizing the reins of change and bending it to your will. Picture a lone wolf traversing the wilderness, encountering obstacles at every turn. Instead of retreating or succumbing to despair, Sigma harnesses their creativity and wisdom gained from unconventional pursuits to conquer the challenges that lay before them.

The Sigma's diverse interests and unconventional knowledge become invaluable assets, often when least expected. What may have begun as a hobby or passing interest transforms into a potent tool for navigating life's ever-changing landscape. Whether mastering graffiti art in the dead of night or tinkering with technology in a garage laboratory, the Sigma's eclectic skill set is akin to a Swiss army knife—ready to tackle any challenge. These seemingly unrelated experiences are not mere pastimes; they are lessons in resilience, resourcefulness, and creative problem-solving.

As we embrace adaptability, we draw upon our wealth of knowledge and wisdom, transforming obstacles into opportunities and thriving amidst uncertainty.

Have you ever found yourself as the sole individual in your group who unravels a solution, solely because you've previously studied or practiced something similar, thereby rescuing the project? For example, my childhood fascination with magic and sleight of hand now aids in detecting deception in my surroundings.

In today's world of constant flux, the ability to quickly adapt is the currency of survival. Sigmas thrive amidst the chaos, standing tall and resolving to conquer whatever challenges come their way. They understand that true power lies in shaping their own destiny, embracing change not as a threat, but as a canvas upon which to paint their dreams and aspirations.

In our exploration of adaptability, we uncover the secrets of Sigma resilience. From leveraging past experiences to embracing failure as a badge of honor, we discover how to thrive in the face of adversity. With grit, determination, and an unwavering belief in our potential, we navigate life's ever-changing landscape with courage and conviction.

Let us continue to embrace adaptability as a weapon in our arsenal—a tool to be wielded with skill and finesse. Let us confront the challenges of tomorrow with creativity, wisdom, and an unshakable belief in our ability to triumph against all odds. As the world continues to spin and twist, let us stand firm, ready to adapt, innovate, and conquer whatever comes our way.

Chapter 9: Navigating Emotional Intelligence: Authenticity Amidst Selectivity

In this crucial chapter, we navigate emotional intelligence through the lens of authenticity and selectivity—a vital aspect of the Sigma mindset. While we recognize the significance of emotions in shaping our interactions, we understand the importance of remaining genuine in our bonds with others, even amidst our selectivity.

Emotional intelligence isn't just about understanding our own feelings; it's about navigating the complexities of human emotions with clarity and discernment. Sigmas embrace authenticity in their connections, fostering genuine relationships based on mutual respect and understanding. However, we remain selective, recognizing that not every bond is worth our energy and investment.

In our journey through emotional intelligence, we acknowledge the harsh reality that not everyone cares about our feelings. It's not about harboring resentment or bitterness but adopting an "it is what it is" attitude toward emotional dysfunction. Some people just ain't shit. Sigmas understand that while conflict and discord are inevitable at times, we have the power to choose what to nurture and what to leave behind.

Furthermore, emotional intelligence empowers us to discern between genuine connections and superficial interactions. This is especially true with Sigma males. We understand that not every relationship serves our growth and well-being, and we have the wisdom to invest our time and energy where it truly matters. Sigmas navigate the delicate balance of authenticity and selectivity with grace and poise, forging meaningful connections while maintaining solid boundaries.

We recognize that genuine bonds enrich our lives and propel us toward growth, while superficial connections drain our energy and hinder our progress. By nurturing authenticity and cultivating selectivity, we empower ourselves to navigate the complexities of human relationships with wisdom and resilience.

Let us now consciously explore the depths of emotional intelligence, even honing our ability to remain authentic amidst selectivity. By embracing the power of discernment, we navigate the intricacies of human connections with clarity and purpose. Embrace authenticity, embrace selectivity, and watch as your relationships flourish and your inner strength grows.

Chapter 10: The Art of Influence: Navigating Leadership as a Sigma

In this chapter, we delve into the essence of leadership as a Sigma—an art form that transcends traditional notions of authority and power. For us, leadership isn't about barking orders or exerting control; it's about inspiring others to act through authenticity, integrity, and vision. Remember those moments when you've stepped up to lead, rally a team toward a common goal, or stand up for something you believe in? That's the essence of Sigma leadership.

Sigmas are natural-born leaders, possessing a unique ability to inspire others without resorting to the tactics of alphas. We lead with confidence, genuine skill, and knowledge, fostering collaboration, empowerment, and growth. Our style is rooted in authenticity and empathy, guiding others with a firm yet compassionate hand.

We excel at connecting with others on a deeper level, intuitively understanding their needs, motivations, and aspirations. This emotional intelligence allows us to tailor our approach to each individual, building trust, loyalty, and respect along the way.

Influence, for Sigmas, is a delicate balance of persuasion and inspiration. It's about articulating a compelling vision and rallying others around it with passion and conviction. We lead from the front, taking calculated risks and embracing failure as a necessary step toward success.

But above all, leadership for Sigmas is about legacy. It's about leaving a lasting impact on the world, inspiring others to reach their full potential and creating a ripple effect that extends far beyond our own lifetime. We understand that true leadership is measured not by ego or followers, but by the depth of our impact and the lives we touch.

As we navigate the complexities of leadership as Sigmas, we remain true to our values and lead with integrity, humility, and relentless commitment to excellence. We embrace our differences, knowing they make us strong, and lead with purpose, passion, and precise conviction.

Paying the cost to be the boss is more than just a mantra—it's a way of life.

We embrace the sacrifices and hardships, knowing they shape us into the leaders we are meant to be. Every setback is an opportunity to prove our strength and resilience, leaving a legacies that will inspire generations to come.

Chapter 11: The Sigma Edge: Unleashing Unparalleled Power

We saved the best for last. In this chapter, we peel back the layers of Sigma superiority, revealing the raw, unadulterated power that courses through our veins. Sigmas aren't just your average Joes—we're the architects of our destinies, the masters of our domains, and the orchestrators of our own damn lives.

We operate on a different wavelength, a frequency reserved for those who dare to defy the status quo and forge their own path. While the world sleeps, we're out here, grinding, hustling, and making shit happen. We don't wait for opportunities to knock—we kick down the damn door and seize them.

Don't fuck with a Sigma. Seriously. We've got skills that'll make your head spin and a strategic mind that's always three steps ahead. We see the chessboard while others are still fumbling with the pieces, and we play to win, no matter the cost.

Our intuition is razor-sharp, our instincts finely honed. We can read people like open books, seeing through their bullshit with a single glance. Manipulation? Please. We wrote the damn playbook.

But it's not just about outsmarting our adversaries; it's about outclassing them in every way possible. We don't stoop to their level—we rise above it, standing tall and proud, knowing that we're the kings of our own castle.

They want to underestimate us. They want to write us off as outsiders, loners, misfits. Let 'em. But just remember, we are the ones they count when the shit hits the fan. It's the Sigma who'll come out on top, when the smoke clears, standing victorious amidst the wreckage, a beacon of strength and resilience in a world gone mad.

In the game of life, there are players and there are spectators. And we, my friends, are the players—the ones who make the rules, break the rules, and rewrite the damn rulebook altogether. Buckle up, buttercup, 'cause the Sigma train is leaving the station, and you'd better believe we're driving this bitch straight to the top.

Made in the USA
Middletown, DE
06 July 2024

56728183R00035